Mind Shifting

Master Your Mindset, Step into Your Power, and Unlock the Secret to Your Success

Life Shifting Series Book One

Nathalie Thompson

Copyright © 2016 by Nathalie Thompson. All rights reserved.

No part of this publication may be reproduced, stored in a retrieval system, or transmitted in any form or by any means – electronic, mechanical, photocopying, recording, scanning, or otherwise – except for brief quotations in critical reviews or articles, without the prior written permission of the author.

The author of this book does not dispense medical advice or prescribe the use of any technique as a form of treatment for physical, emotional, or medical problems without the advice of a licensed physician, either directly or indirectly. Any use of information in this book is at the reader's discretion and risk. The advice and strategies contained herein may not be suitable for your particular situation, and you should always consult with a professional where appropriate. Neither the author nor the publisher shall be liable for any loss, claim, or damage resulting from the use or misuse of the suggestions made.

All trademarks and registered trademarks appearing in this book are the property of their respective owners.

For information visit the author's web sites at:

www.NathalieThompson.com
www.VibeShifting.com.

ISBN: 978-0-9948844-2-8 (ebk)
ISBN: 978-0-9948844-8-0 (pbk)

> "We are what we think.
> All that we are arises with our thoughts.
> With our thoughts we make our world."
> ~Buddha

Table of Contents

Introduction   1

  The Missing Piece   2
  Does Mindset Really Matter?   3
  Minding Your Mind-Talk   4
  What This Book Will Do For You   6

Chapter 1: Uncovering Your Abundance Threshold   9

  Your Abundance-O-Meter   10
  Are You Allergic to Abundance?   11
  Stuck on the Threshold   12
  The Colour of Your Glasses   14
  What Your Filters Do   16
  Everything Starts Within   17
  What's a Mind Shift?   18

Chapter 2: Sidelined By Your Own Beliefs   21

  What's Your Opinion?   22
  The Confession of Your Character   23
  Digging Deeper, Finding Patterns   24
  Beware Your "Yeah But's"   25
  Easier Said Than Done?   26
  Directing Your Focus   27
  Choosing a New Path   28
  Creating Your Own Reality   29

Chapter 3: Dialing Up Your Own Success   31

Clarity is Crucial	32
Tuning In To What You Want	33
Aligning With Your Success	34
Alignment Strategies	35
Making Use of Cosmic Static	40
Chapter 4: Believing in Yourself	43
I Want To Believe (But I Don't)	44
Subconscious Programming	45
What Belief Can Do	46
Your Self-Belief Saboteurs	47
How to Believe In Yourself	48
Your Will Leads to Your Way	51
Chapter 5: Stepping Into Your Power	53
People Just Like You	54
Reprogramming Your Mind	55
Upgrading Your Conviction	56
Powering Up	57
Resetting Your Abundance-O-Meter	58
A Letter to the Reader	61
Other Books By This Author	62
About the Author	63

Introduction

> "Progress is impossible without change, and those who cannot change their minds cannot change anything."
> ~George Bernard Shaw

So you want to make a change in life – like starting a business, losing weight, or changing career paths – but it hasn't been working out for you.

You're doing everything right: you're trying hard, working diligently, and nimbly shifting tactics when you hit roadblocks. You're doing everything you "should" be doing but, for some reason, you're still not getting anywhere with your dreams and goals.

Why, you wonder, is this happening? Or rather, why is it *not* happening for you? After all the blood, sweat, and tears you've poured into this thing, why don't you have anything to show for it yet?

Is it because you're not hustling hard enough despite all the work you're doing? Is it because you don't have the money to pour into fancy tools to make your job easier? Is it because you just don't have the right connections to the right people in the right places to help pave your way to success?

While all of the above might seem like insurmountable barriers to you, the problem isn't actually any of these things. The real reason for all of this crazy-making frustration and lack of results is simply this: it's in your head.

The Missing Piece

So this is usually the part where people get mad and insist that they have *real* obstacles and *real* problems and that these things are most certainly *not* just "in their heads".

Some people will have actually thrown the book down in disgust, vowing never to pick it up again, at the assertion that what's been blocking their success is a product of their minds rather than a clearly defined outside impediment.

But you're still reading.

And that's because there's a part of you that can sense the truth in all of this. Somewhere inside of you, you know that if you're doing all the outward things that other people have done to achieve success, but you're still struggling, then there must be something more to this picture. There must be a missing element or hidden key that you've somehow overlooked and you've reached the point where you're determined to figure out what it is.

And you're right – there is a critical component to this situation that you've been missing up until now. And that's what this book is all about. *Mind Shifting* will help you find that wayward puzzle piece and use it to unlock the final gate between you and whatever it is you want most.

Because here's the big secret: that key that you've been missing up to now is your *mindset*. Your frustration and lack of progress are just by-products of your thought processes. And do you know what? That's a good thing because thought processes can be fixed.

Does Mindset Really Matter?

Is mindset really that big of an issue? Can the thoughts you're thinking really be what's standing between you and your long-sought success?

Absolutely! What's going on in a person's mind is the most important determining factor separating those who successfully build their dreams from those who flounder and fail.

Your mindset matters because your entire experience of life — everything that you will ever do, have, or become — depends on what's going on inside your own head. No matter what you're *doing* on the outside, if what you're *thinking* and *believing* on the inside is knocking your foundation out from under you, you will always find yourself struggling.

Minding Your Mind-Talk

If you want to see a different story outside of you, then you must start with the things you're telling yourself on the inside. And right now the things you're telling yourself are holding you back. Instead of being self-empowering and self-motivating, your internal mind-talk has become self-defeating and self-deterring.

On some level, you have developed a core belief that is preventing you from achieving the kind of success you want with whatever that dream of yours happens to be.

Maybe you secretly believe that:

- "The world is against me."

- "I never get a break."
- "I don't have the right connections."
- "Other people are preventing me from succeeding."

Or maybe you think that the kind of success you dream of is out of reach because:

- "People like me never do anything big."
- "Nobody would ever hire me."
- "Nobody would ever listen to me – I'm just... *me.*"
- "Everyone expects me to fail."

Or maybe it's even something along the lines of:

- "What if I succeed and it changes me?"
- "What if my friends won't like me anymore if I'm successful?"
- "Successful people are self-absorbed snobs. I don't want to be like that!"
- "What if I get everything I want and find out that I don't like it after all?"

These are all examples of self-defeating mind-talk, and these types of thoughts are an indication of your subconscious beliefs about the world and your place within it.

What's underneath all of these beliefs is an *expectation* that you have about how life works. And it is that expectation that determines your likelihood of being successful (or not).

What This Book Will Do For You

Mind Shifting is designed to help you shift those underlying beliefs and expectations. It will help you to stop feeling like a victim of circumstance and start taking control of your life so that you can start building the kind of experience you've always dreamed about.

In my book *fearLESS: How to Conquer Your Fear, Stop Playing Small, and Start Living an Extraordinary Life You Love*, I talked about becoming a Master of Synchronicity and how a change in mindset throws open the doors of your perception. Basically, changing your mindset increases your ability to pick up on all the opportunities that are already out there for you that you never even noticed were there because your old programming, let's call it MindSet 1.0, was actually filtering them out of your field of awareness. You couldn't take advantage of these opportunities because you didn't even *see* them, even when they were right in front of you.

Obviously, if your old programming won't allow you to see the opportunities that are available to you, this is a problem. The old operating system you've been running on has been holding you back. And your mind shift is the equivalent of an upgrade to newer, better,

Introduction

faster software. You're going to find that running this new software, MindSet 2.0, will make everything easier and more transparent from here on in. It creates a simple, but profound shift in the way you operate in the world.

Let me ask you this:

- Do you believe that it is possible for you to achieve your goals and build your biggest dreams in life?
- Do you believe that you deserve to live the kind of life you dream of?
- Do you believe that you have the power to become the kind of person you most want to be?

By the time you've finished *Mind Shifting*, your answer to all of these questions will be a resounding "Hell yes!" and you'll be well on your way to achieving your goals.

By the time you've finished this book you will:

- Understand the mental blocks that are keeping you from the success that you deserve, and what you can do about them.
- Dismantle your subconscious Self-Belief Saboteurs so you can start making real progress towards your goals.

- Reset your Abundance Threshold so that you can easily welcome fantastic success into your life.

In short, *Mind Shifting* is about creating new, success-boosting thought habits so that you can finally get unstuck and start moving forward towards your biggest dreams. It's about giving you the mental tools you need to start building yourself a brand-new reality: the kind of life you've always dreamed of, for yourself and for those you care about most.

Chapter 1: Uncovering Your Abundance Threshold

"ABUNDANCE IS NOT SOMETHING WE ACQUIRE.
IT IS SOMETHING WE TUNE INTO."
~WAYNE DYER

The most important concept you need to understand about making big life changes is what I call your *abundance threshold* – the ingrained, subconscious set point that you have for the good things in life, whatever "the good things" happens to mean to you.

This set point determines how much happiness, wealth, health, creativity, success, etc. that you are able to welcome into your reality. It determines the amount of abundance (of any good thing) that you will allow yourself to have at any given time.

In short, your abundance threshold reflects the amount of abundance that you believe you deserve. You can also think of it as your personal *tolerance level* for success.

Your Abundance-O-Meter

Let's do a little visualization exercise to illustrate this concept a little better: Imagine a room in your mind filled with an enormous, complex machine and banks of fancy, high-tech computer consoles. Stop for a moment and listen to the humming sound it makes and just feel the power that is in this room.

Imagine your gaze being drawn to a particular console with a lever or a dial. As you walk closer to this lever, you see that it marks a setting from "low" to "high", or from "$" to "$$$". This machine is your "Abundance-O-Meter", and it marks the current set point of your abundance threshold. This powerful machine determines how much abundance you are willing to accept into your life. You can handle anything up to the current setting, but any abundance that comes your way that is above this setting will be rejected because the machine is not programmed to accept it.

This is it. This, right here – this simple machine setting is the reason you've been struggling, despite all your efforts to build your dreams.

Think about your life as it currently is. Think about what you've been able to allow into your life so far. Now, look very closely at this machine. Where is your lever currently sitting? Is it at low, medium, or high? How much abundance have you been willing to let yourself enjoy? At what setting are you currently stuck?

For now, all I want you to do is make a note of your current abundance setting, but we're going to come back to this machine later in the book.

Are You Allergic to Abundance?

For those who don't like machines or computers, another way of looking at this is to think of your abundance threshold in terms of an allergy. Think about dust, for example. Did you know that everyone is allergic to dust? For some people, it's just a mild sensitivity and it takes exposure to a large amount of dust before they will react with sneezing and wheezing. For others, there is a true allergy, and even the smallest exposure can trigger allergic reactions.

Just as all people have this dust allergy, every single one of us a similar sensitivity to abundance. Some people can handle a fairly large amount of success, for example, before they start to react to it. For others, even the smallest increase in success exposure will trigger an automated, system-wide response to get rid of the offending "allergen".

As with real allergies, the amount of abundance that each person can handle is different. But for every individual there is a critical threshold that he or she can safely withstand. When the exposure level goes above that threshold, the body's protective mechanisms kick in and the foreign invader is attacked and either destroyed or expelled from the system.

If you have an abundance allergy, any time you expose your system to abundance or success beyond your current threshold limit, you will automatically self-sabotage in order to protect yourself from what you subconsciously believe to be the potentially damaging effects of too much abundance in your life.

Stuck on the Threshold

So everyone has a personal abundance threshold which, when crossed, results in an automatic attempt to get rid of the "dangerous" excess. Occasionally we can spike above our threshold but we inevitably drop back down to that set point again, usually fairly quickly.

Uncovering Your Abundance Threshold

For a lot of people, abundance – in any form – is a scary thing. Too much tends to make people nervous or wary.

Think about it: If you won the lottery today, how would you really feel after the initial, giddy elation wore off? Would you feel absolutely confident about your ability to manage a sudden, vast influx of wealth into your life? Or would you be worried about running out of it, or about how you're going to handle all those distant relatives and nosy neighbours who suddenly want to be your BFF's just so that they can get a piece of the pie? Would you revel in your windfall with joyful gratitude, or would there be a part of you that doubted whether you deserved to have such bounty bestowed upon you with no effort or painful struggle on your part to "earn" it, first?

Your thoughts about this hypothetical situation reflect your existing abundance threshold. And if the life you dream of – the life shift that you want to achieve – is significantly higher than your existing threshold, you will not be able to sustain your success, if you even manage to achieve it at all.

That is, of course, unless you can shift your threshold. If you want a life experience that is significantly beyond what you currently have, you need to push that set point higher so that you are able to easily welcome a greater level of abundance into your life.

If you don't shift your abundance threshold before achieving your success, you'll lose it because you won't be able to tolerate your new level of abundance. Your success antigens will be activated and you will attack and destroy that newfound abundance. You will drop back down to the level that you are used to – the level that you are comfortable with. In other words, you'll find a way to sabotage yourself unless you've already increased your abundance threshold.

The Colour of Your Glasses

If you've ever gone shopping for a new pair of sunglasses, one of the first things you'll notice (aside from the dizzying array of frame styles) is that the lenses come in different colours.

Some sunglasses have orangey-brown lenses, others are more bluish or gray, and still other can be pink or green. And when you try these sunglasses on, you'll notice that the different lens colours affect your view of the world around you. The colour of the lenses you choose actually changes the way you see the objects, spaces and people that come into your field of awareness.

Uncovering Your Abundance Threshold

For example, if you're wearing a pair of orange-lensed glasses, the colour of that lady's sweater looks different than it does when you take the glasses off. The lighting in the store becomes brighter and more orange-y than it does when you're not wearing the glasses.

And if you change to a pair of pink-lensed or blue-lensed glasses, all those things you were looking at change, too. The sweater appears to be yet a different colour, the light changes, even the skin tones of the people around you change. Everything changes based on the colour of the lenses you choose to put on.

This is important because, what if you also happened to be shopping for wallets? And what if the perfect wallet happened to be the exact colour of your lenses? If that was the case, you would miss that wallet completely because it would become invisible to you – it would blend seamlessly into the background because of the filtering effect of your lenses.

Even if that perfect wallet was at the very top of the pile of wallets right in front of you, you would not see it there because your lenses would filter them out of your awareness. Pop those lenses off, however, and that wallet would suddenly appear before you out of nowhere, as if by magic.

What Your Filters Do

It's not magic of course. That wallet was always there – you just couldn't see it because you were filtering it out. That's the way lenses work. And the thing about lenses is they don't have to be "real" in order to have this kind of effect in our lives. In fact, the most potent lenses we have are the ones we wear all the time that we don't even know about. They are the lenses that we create with our thoughts.

These psychological lenses can wreak havoc in our lives because they alter our perception of the world without our even being aware that any filtering effect is even happening. We then make important life decisions and take world-building action based on incomplete or inaccurate information about our situations. And the really scary thing is that we do this constantly. With every breath that we take and every thought that we think we are creating new versions of reality around ourselves.

Right now, right at this very second, you are aligning yourself with a particular version of the world. Everyone is. And creating your life experience this way is not optional – you do it whether you want to or not, whether you think about it or not, whether you try to or not. You create your own reality by default, in every second of your life, based on your existing expectations and preconceptions – based on the psychological filtering lenses that you have put in place. And as you assume that what you perceive through those lenses is your ultimate reality, you create your life around that false perception.

For example, if your mindset has created a belief that the world is a horrible place and bad things always happen to you, you will interpret accidental bumps and bruises as personal affronts and attacks. You will be so focused on simmering resentment of other people's success that you won't even be aware of opportunities before you that might be blatantly obvious to others who have primed themselves to expect good things to happen in life (and whose filtering systems will therefore be on the lookout for those good things).

The problem is that most people aren't aware that they're doing any of this, so they have no control over what they're creating. They assume it's all happening "out there", when in fact it all starts "in here". In a very real way, your life isn't happening *to* you, it's happening *for* you, based on what you have programmed yourself to expect.

Everything Starts Within

Odd though it sounds, your outer reality is a reflection of your inner reality. Essentially, what you experience of the world around you is directly affected by what's happening within you.

As such, any change that you want to make in life has to start within your own mind. Both your greatest obstacles and your greatest assets will all arise from within. They are all based on your beliefs and expectations about yourself and the world around you.

Your expectations, in turn, are based on your beliefs and your beliefs are nothing more than the thoughts you have a *habit* of thinking. These are the thoughts you've had so often over the course of your life that they have become automatic, and often unconscious. And this is the origin of your psychological filtering lenses: they are created and put in place through your thought habits.

What's a Mind Shift?

It is not possible to make an external life shift without first changing those automated internal beliefs and thought habits. In other words, before you can make a life shift you must first change your filtering lenses by making a *mind shift*. You must begin by changing your mind about what you believe is possible – you have to change that mental set point that you've been stuck at.

But making the kind of mindset change necessary to alter your abundance threshold involves a significant, fundamental change in your underlying, core belief systems. In order to create a lasting mind shift, you need to start by identifying and understanding your existing pre-conceptions – those limiting beliefs you have about the world and your place within it that have worked together to create your current abundance threshold.

You need to know what's holding you back before you can take steps to dissolve those mental blocks and open yourself to receiving the universal abundance that is your birthright.

Chapter 2: Sidelined By Your Own Beliefs

"BEGIN CHALLENGING YOUR OWN ASSUMPTIONS. YOUR ASSUMPTIONS ARE YOUR WINDOWS ON THE WORLD. SCRUB THEM OFF EVERY ONCE IN A WHILE, OR THE LIGHT WON'T COME IN."
~ALAN ALDA

In order to dissolve the mental blocks that cause a low abundance threshold, we first need to *find* those blocks. Sometimes they're easy to identify, and sometimes it takes a little self-analysis to figure them out. In all cases, however, your threshold-setting blocks will show up in the way you think, speak, and act.

There is only one real thing that causes the mental blocks that determine your abundance threshold: How you feel and what you believe about the world and your place in it. Your thoughts alone are the determining factor in your experience of life.

What's Your Opinion?

Let me ask you a few simple questions:

- What do you think of the world these days?
- What's your opinion about "most people"?
- When you think about the future of this planet, what do you see?

Now, what was the first thing that came to mind – your automatic reaction – when you first read those questions?

- Did you think the world is a beautiful place, or a horrible place?
- Did you think most people are kind and helpful, or did you think most people are blithering idiots who should never be allowed to breed?
- Did you think the future is full of possibility and wonder, or did you think that everything is going to hell?

Basically, when you think about the world and the people in it, do you think humanity is intrinsically good, or do you think we are inherently bad and, therefore, doomed to self-destruction?

The Confession of Your Character

American Trancendentalist writer Ralph Waldo Emerson once said that: "People seem not to see that their opinion of the world is also a confession of their character."

Think about that for a minute.

I posted the above quote to my blog's Facebook page a while back and one of the comments left by a page fan just said "Ouch, that's harsh…"

Perhaps. But it's also true. What you believe about the world is a reflection of what you carry within. If you believe the world is a cruel, horrible place it is because that's what you *choose* to see in it.

Likewise, if you believe the world to be filled with abundance, joy, and beauty, it's because *that* is what you choose to see in it.

You see the world through filters that *you* put in place, therefore your opinion of the world actually *defines* your own experience of it. In essence you create the world you are experiencing.

What this means is that a negative view of the world should be viewed as an obvious raised flag indicating a low abundance threshold.

Digging Deeper, Finding Patterns

Sometimes the underlying beliefs that determine our abundance thresholds are easy to see, as in the above examples of a negative world view. But sometimes, it takes a little more work to figure out what's holding us back.

If you've been struggling unsuccessfully to make a life shift, you may have noticed some repeating patterns to the events in your life. For example, you may have a tendency to start making progress towards a goal, but then all of a sudden things just go wrong and you find yourself back at square one again, and you have no idea why it keeps happening.

Or perhaps you've noticed that: you keep getting stressed out by the little things; you keep getting sick; you keep winding up in the wrong relationship; you keep losing your job; or you keep procrastinating on doing whatever it is that you need to do in order to create whatever it is that you really want in life.

Repeating, self-sabotaging, patterns like this are another red flag indicating a low abundance threshold.

Beware Your "Yeah But's"

Another way in which you can identify mental blocks is in your default language use when it comes to your dreams and goals.

For example, one of the first things that many people notice when they start looking for their blocks is the "yeah but" habit. You know the one – you or someone else comes up with a great idea that could really propel you forward, but your automatic reaction is "yeah, but..." or "that's great, but..."

So many people have wonderful dreams and goals that they want for themselves. They allow themselves to get all fired up and excited about those dreams for a little bit... and then, for some reason, before they even get started on them, they just let them fizzle out with a defeated "yeah, but...", and that tends to be the end of it.

"I'd like to go back to school, but...", "I'd like to write a book, but...", "I'd like to lose weight, but...", "I'd like to get a new job, but..." and then they never even get started, or they completely give up at the first sign of an obstacle.

If they had only kept going and actually started taking action – if they had only focused on the worlds of possibility before them – they could have done it. But they let the voices of doubt and negativity take over, instead.

A habit of frequently saying "yeah but..." is a sign of a low abundance threshold.

Easier Said Than Done?

Another habit that many people fall into is the "easier said than done" habit. You know this one, too. It's the one where someone gives you a great suggestion (or, you know, you read something important in a self-help book, for example...) and your automatic response is to roll your eyes and say "it's easy to *say* that, but it's not so easy to *do*!"

Well guess what? That kind of thinking is yet another big red flag indicating a low abundance threshold.

The belief that making a mindset change is hard is just that – a belief. And beliefs, as we've seen, are just thoughts that you have made a habit of thinking. So all you need to do is change those underlying thoughts and you can create a brand-new habit for yourself.

By defaulting to the "easier said than done" mentality, you're reinforcing a subconscious belief that what you want is unlikely to happen and you're training yourself to expect difficulties and roadblocks and ongoing problems of all sorts. Why do that to yourself?

Directing Your Focus

If you're trying to build big dreams and amazing things in your life, these counterproductive thought patterns like "yeah but" and "easier said than done" are not the kind of mindset you want to get yourself stuck in. Seemingly innocent little thoughts like these end up negatively colouring our entire worldview and programming our subconscious minds into believing that what we want is impossible.

These thought habits are an indicator of where your focus in life happens to be. Again, your focus determines your expectations. And your expectations determine your reality.

In other words, what we focus on in life is what expands in our experience of it. So will you choose to focus on what you want to see and build and experience in life, or will you choose to focus on all the reasons why you think you can't do any of those things?

Are you programming yourself to look for the possibilities and opportunities that are all around you? Or are you running on auto-pilot and always expecting the worst?

Choosing a New Path

When you default to "easier said than done" or "yeah but", you will find yourself on the road to mediocrity and broken dreams. Why not choose a different path instead? One that says your dreams are possible and that you *will* get there?

"Yeah but" and "easier said than done" are just roundabout ways of looking for reasons to stay in the darkness rather than looking for reasons to expand the light. These phrases are keeping you stuck with a low abundance threshold, and they are blocking your success.

If you want to start dissolving these kinds of blocks, the best thing you can do to is to drop your habit of coming up with excuses as to why you can't have what you want in life. In fact, drop "yeah but" and "easier said than done" from your vocabulary entirely! Reject the *possible* reality of the "yeah, but" (it's only *one* possibility) and choose, as *MythBusters* star Adam Savage once said, to substitute your own.

When you find yourself saying "yeah but", or thinking that something is easier said than done, try to deliberately flip your perspective and tell yourself this, instead: "It's just as easy done as said." It's a much better mindset to get stuck in.

Creating Your Own Reality

What I'm saying is that, if you're going to create your world anyway, then maybe it's time to put some thought into what you want to experience, rather than just doing it on auto-pilot and having to deal with the fallout as you go along.

In other words, if you want to change the way you *experience* the world, you need to change the way you *think* about the world, first. You need to alter the conditioning you've been subjected to.

So tomorrow morning when you wake up, ask yourself again: what do you think of the world today? Or, more specifically: what will you *make* the world today?

And then start small: decide that, just for today, you will make it a point to look for the good in the world. Decide that you will create a world of kindness and love, of possibility and abundance. Then ask yourself the same question again tomorrow.

Choosing what you *want* to focus on has the effect of changing the colour of your glasses. It starts to alter those psychological filters you've been wearing and allows you to start seeing the world as you want it to be. It opens your perception to *possibility*.

Chapter 3: Dialing Up Your Own Success

> "You live out the confusions until they become clear."
> ~Anaïs Nin

So now you know why your mindset is so import to building dreams. But the question still remains: *How* do you create a lasting mind shift that will allow you to reset your abundance threshold so you can welcome the success that's been waiting for you into your life?

There are really only two things that you need to do in order to achieve all of this:

1. Align yourself with what you want.
2. Believe in your ability to get it.

That's it – just two little things. But those two things trip so many people up. In this chapter, we're going to look at how to create alignment. In the next chapter, we'll go in-depth with self-belief strategies.

Clarity is Crucial

Before we dive into our alignment strategies, it's important to understand that everything *starts* with being clear about what you want in the first place.

It sounds so simple and so obvious, but clearly tuning in to what you want is something that trips up even the savviest conscious creators sometimes.

Here's the thing: if you don't know what it is that you want, then how the heck are you going to be able to create it? If you don't even know what your target is, how to do you expect to be able to hit it? You must know what it is that you actually want in life before you will ever be able to live it.

And crystal clarity in this respect is crucial. If your vision isn't clear, then you must ask yourself what your creative energy is centred on. If you "sort of" know what you want, then what you will end up creating is "sort of" what you were after.

In other words, if your focus is blurry, so will your outcomes be.

Tuning In To What You Want

Think of it like a radio – remember those pre-digital models where you had to turn the little knob to tune in to the station you wanted? As you got closer to the station signal, you would start to hear the music, but it would be laced with static, and you would sometimes get input from other stations overlaid on top of what you wanted.

Manifesting the success that you want in life works the same way. As you "sort of" get close to the right signal, you "sort of" get the channel you want. It's only when you're tuning in to the *exact* signal that you get what you really wanted.

You could, of course, just randomly twist the knob around and tune into whatever channel you happen to stumble over, and what you'll get is a bunch of random results. This is how most people create their realities: by random chance, and always wondering why they never really feel satisfied with their lives, or feeling that something is "missing", but never quite knowing what.

You can't stop creating (tuning your "reality station"); it's just what we humans *do*. But you can learn to deliberately create that reality rather than just settling for whatever you happen to find. Once you *know* that what you want is classic rock, for example, you can tune in to that particular station, avoiding the hip hop, jazz, and pop stations that you *don't* want.

And once you know what you want your life to look like, you can concentrate on creating that specific reality for yourself, clearly and without static-y interference from "sort of".

Aligning With Your Success

So the critical thing about manifesting anything in life is this whole tuning in process. It's all a matter of getting yourself into *alignment* with whatever it is that you want. But what does that mean, exactly? And how the heck are you supposed to do it?

When you're in alignment with something, it means that you're a vibrational match to having it happen – it means that everything in you is completely ready to actually have what you want show up in your life.

Keep in mind that, just because you really *want* something, it doesn't mean that you're *ready* for it to happen in your reality. This is important, because when you're having problems manifesting something it usually means that, at some level, you are experiencing resistance to whatever it is you want.

I cover the topic of resistance in depth in my book *fearLESS*, but for now, just know that resistance usually happens because, on some level, you're afraid of the possible downsides to what you want. It means that there is something inside of you that doesn't want to deal with some aspect of whatever it is that you think you want.

For example, you could be thinking that losing all that weight would mean you would never be able to eat your favourite food again, or that if you finally had the perfect relationship, it would mean that you'd have to give up your freedom and ability to do what *you* want to do in life. Those elements that you *don't* want are often strong enough to shift your vibrational alignment into *not* manifesting what you say you want.

Alignment Strategies

So how do you get yourself through that stuff and still get yourself into that all-important alignment with the kind of success you really want? Here are some strategies that can help:

1. *Assume it's a given.*

Worrying about what you want or being afraid that it won't happen just keeps you focused on the fact that what you want is still lacking from your life. As we mentioned earlier in the book, what you focus on is what you tend to bring about in life, so you need to shift the focus away from "it's not here yet" and onto "it's coming" or even "it's here".

Try to think of manifesting what you want as hitting the print button on a printer, or ordering something from an online shop. Getting clear on what you want to manifest is like hitting the "go" button. Once you've placed your order or sent your print job, do you worry that it's not going to come? No, because you *know* that it will. It's just a matter of waiting for it to arrive.

Get yourself into the habit of thinking about the things and experiences that you want to manifest in life in this same manner – once you've sent that desire out into the Universe, *assume* that you've placed your order and that it's already on its way and allow yourself to feel that lovely anticipation of waiting for your parcel to arrive.

2. Get happy.

When we are stressed or unhappy or fretful, it messes up our vibe. It's hard to manifest fun, happy things into your life when your dominant energy pattern is the opposite of that. So, beyond feeling good about what you want, just focus on feeling good in general. Be happy. Do some art, listen to your favourite music, call a friend you haven't talked to in a while, or go for a walk.

Dialing Up Your Own Success

Just take the time to do things that make your heart sing. Feeling wonderful as often as you can is the best way to bring more wonderful things into your life. Start allowing yourself to feel fabulous. Give yourself permission to laugh and play and relax a little! Life is really not meant to be that serious and stressful.

If you're in a difficult situation this can be tough, but start small – get yourself a pack of brand-new crayons just for you and let yourself have fun with colours for a few minutes every day. Splurge on some fresh flowers to brighten up your home next time you're at the grocery store. Or just take a few minutes whenever you can to truly appreciate the little things that you do have in life because it primes your psychological filters to align with more things to appreciate – like greater success and abundance!

3. Visualize it.

Make a movie in your mind and live your life as if what you want is already yours. Imagine every detail with as much clarity as you can and put yourself in the picture. What does your life look like now that you've lost the weight, gotten the job, met "the one", launched your successful business, or been accepted into that elite program? If you can't even *imagine* it happening for yourself, then how can you expect to have it happen in your reality?

Spend five minutes every day visualizing your ideal, perfectly manifested life, in all its wonderful glory. You can spend up to ten minutes, but don't go more than that (use a timer if you need to) – your life is meant to be lived, and actual action is necessary for turning your visions into reality. Don't spend all your time daydreaming, or that's all those visions of yours will ever be. Get yourself jazzed with your visualization practice then get yourself moving!

4. Feel it.

What are the emotions or feelings that you think having what you want will bring you? Remember that it's never really about the things or experiences that we want in life – it's always about how we think those things and experiences will make us *feel*. Get clear about what those underlying feelings are and then find ways to feel them now, before whatever you want has even happened. Professional actors manage to make themselves feel completely different things on cue every single day and so can you.

For example, if you've decided that getting that new job will make you feel respected, then find ways to feel respected now, and start with yourself. Do things that make you respect yourself – hit the treadmill and work on increasing your endurance a little bit more every week and feel respect for the dedication you put into it. Take a plastic bag with you next time you go for a walk and pick up some trash along the way, and feel the respect for an individual who takes pride in his surroundings and cares for the people and places most important to him. Remember the times in your life when you have already felt respected and add those to your visualization routine.

5. Act as if.

Start behaving as if what you want is already here. There are different ways in which you can do this. For example, you can start assuming the identity of the person you're hoping to become.

In other words, if you've got a day job as an accountant but you dream about being an internationally acclaimed stand-up comic, then start telling people you are a comedian. When asked what you do for a living, answer that you are a comedian. If that feels "off" to you – if the thought of saying that makes you feel like you'd be lying – then say you're in the process of launching your career in stand-up and that you do accounting on the side.

You can also start creating space for the thing that you want in your life so that there's room for it when it does arrive. For example, if what you want is a new relationship then start sleeping on "your" side of the bed, clear out a dresser drawer for Mr. or Ms. Right's use and figure out where his or her towel is going to get hung up in the bathroom. If you've got your heart set on a new car, then clear out your garage so there's room for your new ride!

Another way to "act as if" that I've talked about on my blog is to completely put yourself in the mindset of already being, having, or experiencing what you want. So, if you want to make your business financially successful, then ask yourself how a woman with a financially successful business would answer her phone or fold her laundry. How would the guy who successfully finished his first triathlon order dinner or vacuum his floor? Get yourself completely into the persona of having already achieved what you want to, and BE that person in every aspect of your life, both large and small, in whatever ways you can.

Give these alignment tricks a try and start shifting your mindset and energy into the right place for making it happen!

Making Use of Cosmic Static

One final thought: if you are muddling through some "cosmic static" with your tuning process and are only managing to manifest "sort of" what you want into your life, don't look at it as a bad thing! "Sort of" means you're in the right general area, vibrationally speaking, to create what you want. Look at "sort of" as evidence that you are getting closer to what you want, and use it to fine tune your focus with this formula:

"I like [*this* aspect] of this manifestation, but I want it to have more [whatever it is you want]!"

For example:

- "I really like the layout of the kitchen in the house we just looked at, but I want it to have a walk-in pantry, too."
- "I love the creative aspects of this job, but I want more freedom to make decisions on my own, too."
- "I really enjoy being my own boss, but I want to find clients more easily, too."

Use the contrast to help you get clearer about your vision and desires, get yourself really focused on what you want, and you'll be on track to building your biggest dreams and creating the kind of life you most want for yourself!

Chapter 4: Believing in Yourself

> "IT'S NO GOOD BEING TOO EASILY SWAYED
> BY PEOPLE'S OPINIONS.
> YOU HAVE TO BELIEVE IN YOURSELF."
> ~DONATELLA VERSACE

In the previous chapter you learned that there are two keys to making a lasting mind shift, and you got a lot of strategies to help with the first key: clarity. In this chapter we're going to take a look at the second key: self-belief.

The core mantra with my work at VibeShifting.com is that "If you can dream it and believe it, you can always achieve it!", and I believe that 100%. But how do you get that first part down? How do you find ways to start believing in yourself when you just... don't?

This is super-important because without nailing down the self-belief component of mind shifting, it won't matter how much clarity you have about what you want: if you don't believe in yourself, you won't be strong enough to weather the storms that come with building any important-to-you dream.

I Want To Believe (But I Don't)

I got a message from someone on Twitter once who wanted to know how to maintain unshakeable belief in herself and her dreams. It was the one thing she felt would make everything else easier to deal with.

I think it's a sentiment we all understand. It's so important to believe in ourselves, but what so often happens is that the voices of doubt – both inside and outside of us – take hold and undermine that belief. We put more stock in the negative than we do in the positive.

I discussed the reasons for this in my book *Simple Strategies for Stress Relief*, and the quick version is that our brains are hardwired to pay more attention to negative stuff and to downplay the importance of positive stuff, because the positive stuff is harmless, but the negative stuff could be dangerous. The technical term for this is *negativity bias*.

Subconscious Programming

The other confounding factor with the whole problem of negativity bias is that so many of us are also fighting a lifetime of programming that tells us that that our dreams are impossible.

How many of the following phrases have you heard in your lifetime?

- "That's impossible. It'll never happen."
- "Stop kidding yourself."
- "Who do you think you are?!"
- "It's a nice hobby, but no one ever makes any money at it."
- "Stop being so selfish and just be grateful for what you have!"

All of these phrases, and the thousands more like them that we've been listening to all our lives, have had the effect of programming our subconscious minds to stop believing in our dreams and abilities. And all of this programming continues to sabotage our self-belief into adulthood.

This is problematic because when you don't believe that you *can* achieve your goals and you don't believe that you *deserve* to achieve them, you're pretty much setting yourself up for guaranteed failure.

What Belief Can Do

On the flip side, however, learning how to improve self-belief – and maintain it – can provide you with all sorts of benefits:

- You are less dependent on external validation, becoming more emotionally stable and less likely to get drawn into that roller-coaster ride where your thoughts about yourself and your abilities are based on what other people say to you or about you at any given time.
- You are better able to silence your own inner critic, and are more likely to achieve your goals because you are more willing to take action.
- Your relationships with other people will be smoother and more pleasant because people are naturally drawn to those who are confident. In addition, those who have high self-esteem are happier, less needy, and more pleasant to be around than those who aren't.

Believing in yourself will help improve all areas of your life, but how do you do it?

Your Self-Belief Saboteurs

The first step in learning how to believe in yourself is to become aware of your *self-belief saboteurs*. These are the ingrained patterns of thinking that we develop over the course of a lifetime that cause us to have a really distorted view of the world around us.

These negative thought patterns can take many forms, including:

- **Seeing things in black and white.** This is the tendency to view things from an all-or-nothing, all good or all bad, kind of framework. This one tends to show up in the form of "If I don't get that job, I'm a failure" or "If I don't get an A on this test, I'm an idiot".
- **Dwelling on the negative.** This is the tendency to focus only on the bad stuff, constantly worrying about it and reliving it until it's all you can even see anymore.
- **Jumping to conclusions.** This is the tendency to view yourself negatively as the cause of someone else's behaviour, with little or no evidence. (e.g. You texted your friend and she still hasn't responded so you assume she's mad at you.)

How to Believe In Yourself

Learning to deprogram yourself and rebuild your self-confidence after a lifetime of negativity is possible. But you're going to have to change your automated thought habits and that does take dedication and resolve.

Here's how you can get started:

Tip #1: Surround yourself with positive people.

One of the most important things you can do is to surround yourself with the kinds of people who will support your dreams and goals. Find people who have their own dreams and who are working to build something better with their own lives, because their energy and attitudes will rub off on you.

The corollary to this, of course, is that you also need to minimize the time you spend around those negative people who seem to get off on shooting down other people's dreams and ideas (we all know people like this), because their energy and attitudes will just bring you down.

You don't need to cut the Debbie Downers out of your life completely because – let's face it – some of the most negative people we know are often friends or even family. This makes total avoidance both impractical and undesirable. Having a positivity buffer of positive influencers around you to counteract the unavoidable negativity in your life is, therefore, critical.

Tip #2: Focus on your successes.

Make a list of every great thing you've accomplished in your life – everything you've done that you've ever been proud of, or excited about. If you can't think of any, then ask one of your positive-people friends what they think some of your greatest accomplishments are, or ask them what they think your greatest strengths are.

Write it all down and refer to this list often to focus your mind on the fact that you *have* had wonderful success in the past – it will help to program your mind into believing that you can create more success in the future.

Tip #3: Look at failure as a friend.

Most people fear failure. It is such a common fear that I've got an entire chapter devoted to it in *fearLESS*. But failure is not your enemy, it's just part and parcel of your learning curve; it's a necessary and completely inevitable part of building your dream.

Start viewing success as a process... one in which there will be many failures, many rejections, and many "NO"s. Every time a door gets closed, though, learn to see it as a sign that there is obviously a better way or a better road to get you to where you want to go. A roadblock doesn't mean the trip is over... it means you haul out your map and find a different route!

Tip #4: Flip your funks.

When you start doubting yourself and thoughts like "I can't do this" or "What if it doesn't work?" start floating through your mind, catch yourself and stop for a moment. These are automated thought habits kicking in, and this is a chance to start reprogramming yourself in a better way.

If you start thinking that you can't do something, then flip it around and say to yourself "I can't do this *yet*, but I can totally learn how!" If you're worried that something might not work out, then tell yourself "Well, if this doesn't work out, then I'll try again another way!" Don't get stuck in your funks – flip them around into something positive!

Tip #5: Stretch your comfort zone.

Comfort zones are... well, *comfortable,* and trying to move out of yours is scary. But getting yourself out of the "same old, same old" routine is the *only* way that you will ever be able to build your dreams. Remind yourself that even if you're scared, at least you're *doing* something.

Thomas Jefferson once said that "If you want something you've never had, you must be willing to do something you've never done." Start small... do one little thing that scares you (make one cold call or send an email to a potential resource or client, for instance) and edge yourself out of your comfort zone.

If you can get yourself to do something scary, despite your heart palpitations, you'll quickly learn that you can survive the fear, and that after it's done, it wasn't as bad as you thought it would be. Keep pushing your comfort zone boundaries, just a little bit, on a consistent basis and you'll start believing that you can accomplish anything you set out to!

Your Will Leads to Your Way

Learning how to believe in yourself is critical because if you don't believe that something is possible, you will never commit yourself to making it happen.

When you do believe it's possible, then nothing is going to stop you. Every roadblock and every hiccup you encounter will only serve to steel your resolve and spur you on to greater heights of creativity and ingenuity. You will become the poster child for the phrase "where there's a will, there's a way".

Chapter 5:
Stepping Into Your Power

> "DON'T DOWNGRADE YOUR DREAM JUST TO
> FIT YOUR REALITY. UPGRADE YOUR CONVICTION
> TO MATCH YOUR DESTINY."
> ~STUART SCOTT

So now you know what your abundance threshold is and how it's been keeping you stuck at a less-than-stellar level of success. You've learned how your automatic thoughts and psychological filters have created this set point, and you've learned the two keys to changing those thought habits and dialing up your own success.

Now you're ready to use this information to consciously create your ideal reality and welcome the success you've been wanting into your life for good. It's time for you to step into your power and make your mind shift.

People Just Like You

At the beginning of this book we talked about the self-defeating mind-talk that so many of us subject ourselves to on a daily basis, beliefs like "people like me never do that..." This is the belief that our particular circumstance or background is enough to prevent us from ever achieving our goals or living our biggest dreams.

But know this: People like you are creating amazing things every day. People in situations just like yours are turning things around. At this very moment, people just like you are waking up to their own power and building great dreams.

And you have that potential for greatness inside of you right now, too. You have unique experience and insights that someone else is looking for. You have abilities and talents that have the potential to change your entire world. You just need to let them out and put them to use.

If you want something badly enough, and are willing to work for it, you can have it. You just need to convince yourself of that, and the rest will come. Never sell yourself short by believing in the haters. The only people who want you to fail are people who have already failed themselves and given up on what's most important to them. And unless you want to end up bitter and jaded just like them, you need to stop listening to them and start working on your own dreams. And you need to start today.

Reprogramming Your Mind

Start by programming your mind to look for all the ways in which your dreams could come true rather than fearing all the ways in which they can't. Make it an exercise: brainstorm a list of all the ways in which you could achieve your goals. Write down any ideas that come to mind, no matter how crazy or far-fetched they seem to your logical mind. The point of brainstorming is simply to record the ideas as they flow.

Need money to buy a certain piece of software for your business, for example? Maybe it could fall out of the sky into your lap! Don't laugh – my kids and I once walked around a corner to find a whole bunch of money blowing along the street. We picked up over $100 with not a soul in sight anywhere around us to whom it could have belonged, so expand your mind. Be open to every possibility and don't place arbitrary limits on how you believe things *should* happen. Be clear about your goals, but be flexible in how they are achieved.

Start training yourself to look for and work for the positive in life. Start moving towards that dream and focus on what you *can* do, today, to bring yourself even the tiniest bit closer to your dream (and there is *always* something that you can do). Just start moving and let inertia work its magic on your behalf. An object in motion tends to stay in motion, after all!

Your reality is what you choose to create. Just because someone else says it's not possible, or wasn't able to do it themselves, does not mean that you will also fail. Look beyond the surface and start seeing things differently. It doesn't have to be hard (unless you believe it has to be). And sometimes the simplest things make the biggest difference in our mindset.

Upgrading Your Conviction

It's so easy to fall into the trap of comparing where we are to where we *want* to be and then getting completely disheartened by how far we still have to go. Don't fall into this trap. It's not about where you are, it's about knowing where you're going to be. It's about upgrading your conviction and beliefs to match your vision of the future.

When you upgrade your conviction, you're making a commitment to yourself that you will do whatever it takes to make your dream a reality. You're accepting responsibility for your own success or failure and you're placing the first metaphysical domino to set off a cascade of events that will ultimately result in a brand-new reality.

Powering Up

So now we have reached the point where you must decide: do you want this dream of yours or not? Are you ready to step into your power and create the reality you desire? Are you prepared to begin your own quest for greatness? Are you ready to become all that you know you are capable of becoming?

Ask yourself one simple question: what's it worth to you? In other words, how badly do you want it and what are you willing to do to get it? Think about what your life will be like a year from now if you don't make that dream of yours happen. And then think about what it could be like if you did. Pick the reality you prefer and decide that it *will be.*

When you make a decision, and when you can feel a sense of inevitability about it, *that* is when the magic starts to happen. It starts with that internal, gut-level, feeling of certainty. And you are the only one who has the power to forge that internal alchemy. The power is yours, but you must *choose* to use it. As we said in the previous chapter: your will leads to your way.

You already have everything within you that you need in order to make your life shift happen. All those outer things will come once you've made the mind shift necessary to completely align yourself with your goal. As Mother Teresa once said, "The first step to becoming is to will it."

Resetting Your Abundance-O-Meter

Go back for a moment to our thought experiment from chapter 2, back to that room in your mind where your "Abundance-O-Meter" is humming along. Do you remember what your machine was set to when you started this book?

Now that you have learned all this stuff, has your setting changed at all? Where is the dial sitting now? For most people, the information in this book will have shifted their setting toward greater abundance – but only a little.

What I'm going to ask you to do now, however, is to deliberately shift that setting even further. I want you to imagine yourself reaching out to the dial. Feel yourself grabbing a hold of it. Think about your now-clear vision of what you want. Think about how much you believe in your ability to make it happen (or at least think about what it would feel like if you did believe in yourself).

Stepping Into Your Power

Now crank that dial all the way to "high" or "$$$" – and then lock it down. Reset your abundance threshold as high as you now feel comfortable setting it and imagine it clicking into place at this new, higher setting. Take a moment to really feel the excitement and satisfaction of powering up that abundance setting, and what it means for your life from here on in.

It may be symbolic, but never underestimate the power of symbolism on your subconscious mind. You have just sent yourself a powerful internal message that you are ready to accept greater abundance and success into your life. You are now ready to take your life to the next level in your personal evolution.

You have just made your own mind shift. And you have opened yourself up to a whole new world of possibility. This is the key that you were missing. And with this element now in place, nothing can hold you back from the life you want to live. You can now create, and more importantly *accept*, the kind of life you've always wanted. You are now ready to live your dreams...

A Letter to the Reader

Dear Reader,

I hope you enjoyed *Mind Shifting*. Thank you so much for taking time out of your busy schedule to read it!

As you know, reviews are the lifeblood of any book – especially for us indie authors. Without them, our books quickly disappear from book store search algorithms and fade into obscurity. And that makes the books very, very sad.

If you'd like to help make this particular book very, very happy, it would be thrilled if you could leave it a review. You can do that right here:

(Just scan the QR code, and then click the "Write a Customer Review" button at the bottom of the page). Thanks so much, from both me and my book, and have a fantastic day!

> Light and love,
> Nathalie Thompson

Other Books By This Author

The Positive Affirmations Handbook
fearLESS

The Life Shifting Series:

Mind Shifting
Soul Shifting
Body Shifting (Coming Soon!)

The Simple Strategies Series:

Simple Strategies for Stress Relief
Simple Strategies for Mindfulness

Coloring Books:

Mystical Mantras Coloring Book
Celtic Knots Coloring Book

Want to be the first to know when new books are published?
Sign up for the author's newsletter at www.NathalieThompson.com!

About the Author

Nathalie Thompson wants to live in a world where coffee pots are never empty and everyone is living the extraordinary life of their dreams.

A transformation catalyst and motivational expert, she is the author of *fearLESS* and *Mind Shifting* and her articles have been featured on the *Huffington Post* and on the blogs of NYT best-selling inspirational authors Pam Grout and Mike Dooley.

Connect with her and start transforming *your* dreams into reality over at www.VibeShifting.com!

/vibeshifting @vibeshifting

Made in the USA
Monee, IL
12 January 2025